IMAGES OF
SCOTLAND

Karen Fitzpatrick has worked in book publishing for many years, some of which she spent in London. She now lives in her native Scotland with her family and works as an editor and writer. Her particular areas of interest include Scottish culture and literature.

This is a **FLAME TREE** book
Created for Lomond

FLAME TREE PUBLISHING

Crabtree Hall, Crabtree Lane
Fulham, London SW6 6TY
www.flametreepublishing.com

Flame Tree is part of the Foundry Creative Media Company Limited

Thanks to: Mike and Carl at V.K. Guy, Vanessa Green, Chelsea Edwards, Chris Herbert, Julie Pallot, Frances Bodiam and Nick Wells

IMAGES OF
SCOTLAND

KAREN FITZPATRICK

LOMOND

CONTENTS

THE HEBRIDES, ORKNEY AND SHETLAND ISLES

The remoteness and the rugged beauty of the islands off
the northern coast of Scotland are what make them so
magical. Stone circles, castles, ruined abbeys and thriving
fishing villages all mixed up with the power of nature
and the allure of the soft lull of the gaelic language,
make these islands unique and unforgettable. Over the
next few pages, the beautiful photography brings the
essence of these islands to life.

Standing Stones of Callanish

LEWIS

The Standing Stones of Callanish on the Isle of Lewis are among the largest stone settings in the UK. Erected between 3,000 and 4,000 years ago their purpose is shrouded in mystery, and is intensified by the haunting yet spectacular landscape. A complex arrangement of 50 stones, with an inner circle of 13 stones (and a burial tomb in its centre), its shape forms a Celtic cross. Long associated with astrology and the lunar cycle, perhaps the most interesting, if not the most whimsical, explanation belongs to Lewis folklore: that in a bid to convert giants to Christianity, they were turned to stone by St Kieran.

Tolsta Head

LEWIS

On the east coast, north of Stornoway, are the most breathtaking beaches on the Isle of Lewis. With immaculately clean crystal waters, pure white sand and a rocky coastline they exude postcard-prettiness. Although tranquil, the beaches are massively populated, not with people (thankfully!), but with a diverse wildlife. Tolsta Head in particular is home to many species of birds, seals, dolphins, porpoises and occasionally whales, which are sometimes seen close to the shore.

Seilebost

HARRIS

The Norse meaning for Harris is 'high land' and the area is often described as the 'high heart of the Hebrides'. With such an abundance of natural beauty – high mountains, sea lochs, coastal islands, sandy white beaches (like Seilebost pictured here) as well as the typically Scottish ruggedness of the slate grey rock and prickly green heather – it is no wonder. The Harris Hills, of which the highest is Clisham at 799 m (2621 ft), are formed from the oldest rock on the planet and have a striking similarity to the surface of the Moon.

Portree

SKYE

Portree derives from the Gaelic *Port-an-Righ*, meaning 'King's Port'. It earned this name in 1540 when King James V and his army of men arrived on the island looking for the support of the clans. As Skye's main town, Portree's harbour, with its pretty coloured fishing boats, is the centre of the community. Behind the harbour lies Bank Street, most famous for the Royal Hotel, which in 1746 was MacNab's Inn, and was where Flora MacDonald bid farewell to Bonnie Prince Charlie after smuggling him 'Over the Sea to Skye'.

Neist Point

SKYE

The most westerly point on the Isle of Skye, Neist Point offers superb vistas beyond Moonen Bay right over to the Western Isles, and has a spectacular 19 m-high (62 ft) lighthouse, which was built in 1909. The distinctive rock formation of the shore-line around Neist Point is just like that of the Giant's Causeway in Northern Ireland, and local story-telling lays claim that the causeway travels all the way under the sea from Northern Ireland and rises up again at Neist Point on the Isle of Skye.

The Cuillin

FROM SLIGACHAN, SKYE

The sheer rugged beauty of the spiked peaks of the Black Cuillin hills can be seen from most vantage points around Skye (pictured here from Sligachan). The Black Cuillin are composed of basalt and gabro, and are the most challenging climb in the UK. Also, all of the 12 Munros on Skye are Black Cuillin peaks and breathtaking, far-reaching views can be found from their tops. Less well-known are the Red Cuillin hills (composed of granite rock, giving them a reddish shade), which are lower and less rocky.

Castle Moil

KYLEAKIN, SKYE

Castle Moil, or in gaelic *Caisteal Maol*, dates back to the tenth century, and is situated close to the village of Kyleakin's harbour and opposite to the Skye Bridge. Now almost completely ruined, the castle at one time served as a lookout post and fortress. Run by a Norwegian princess, known as 'Saucy Mary', she levied a toll on all ships travelling the narrow sound between Skye and the mainland, and even went as far as stretching a length of chain across the water to stop any boats from avoiding payment.

Torosay Castle

MULL

Built in 1858 in the Scottish baronial style by the Scottish architect David Bryce (1803–76), Torosay Castle is still used as a family home (on the upper floors). The main rooms of the mansion are open to the public with the likes of a portrait of William Wallace (c. 1270–1305), Loch Ness monster memorabilia and photographs of Winston Churchill (1874–1965) (who often visited in his younger years) on display. The castle is famed for its impressive 12-acre gardens, which offer formal Italianate terraces, informal woodland and an impressive statue walk with 19 life-size limestone figures.

Tobermory

MULL

The main street of Tobermory, with its quirky, brightly painted houses that wrap around the peaceful bay, is what most people associate with Mull's capital. With a population of around 700, it tends to be a peaceful place – that is until it hits summer season when a mass pilgrimage of young Cbeebies' *Balamory* fans hit the island. The TV show, which centres around Tobermory's colourful houses, has seen Mull's tourist industry sky rocket. For resistant parents, there is always the draw of the 1588 Spanish Armada's treasure of gold, which is believed by some to be buried deep in the waters of Tobermory's harbour.

Iona Abbey

IONA

Iona has been a place of Christian pilgrimage since AD 563, when Iona Abbey was founded by St Columba and his Irish followers, and attracts approximately 140,000 worshippers every year. Iona Abbey was restored over a century ago and is among Scotland's most sacred and historical sites. Of particular interest are the abbey church and cloister, the shrine and writing cell of St Columba and some 180 medieval stones and crosses. In the Abbey's graveyard lie many early Scottish, Irish, Norwegian and French Kings.

Kiloran Bay

COLONSAY

Kiloran Bay, an inlet on the north-west coastline of the tiny island of Colonsay, is one of the most beautiful beaches in Scotland. The natural resources of this fertile machair are believed to have been of great attractiveness to early Viking settlements and, although no settlement site has been found, in 1882 a Viking boat grave was discovered (the grave dating between AD 875 and 925) with the remains of a Viking man, his horse, his weapons and other everyday objects.

Isle of Orsay

NEAR PORTNAHAVEN, ISLAY

Portnahaven and its neighbour Port Wemyss are situated at the very north of Islay on a peninsula that forms around the north side of Loch Indaal. Portnahaven is the more beautiful of the two villages with an array of picturesque white cottages and a lovely harbour. Facing the village of Port Wemyss is the Isle of Orsay (pictured here) with its striking lighthouse, which was built by Robert Stevenson (1772–1850) in 1825.

St Ninian's Isle

SHETLAND

St Ninian's Isle is a small island – inhabited only by sheep – that joins the south-western coast of mainland Shetland and, unless the tide is very high, it is possible to walk across the sand from the mainland. Considered a holy island, it is dedicated to St Ninian, who is considered by locals as Shetland's patron saint. A small ruined chapel is located on the island where several Neolithic graves were found as well as a hoard of silver treasure, dating back to AD 800, which was discovered by a young schoolboy who was helping at an archaeological dig in 1958.

Ring of Brodgar

ORKNEY

Only 27 of the original 60 stones that form this stone ring remain, and they rise starkly out of the thin piece of land that lies between Stenness Loch and Harray Loch. As of yet the date of the ring's construction is not yet known, as the site has not been fully excavated. Scientists, however, believe that work on this ceremonial monument began between 3000 BC and 2000 BC and that it was part of a massive circle complex, of which the Standing Stones of Stenness (one mile to the east of the Ring of Brodgar) would have been a part of.

Yesnaby Sea Stack

ORKNEY

Some of the most spectacular scenery in the world is to be found on Orkney. Yesnaby, in particular, is one of the most breathtaking places on the islands, and inlets and sea stacks have been formed from the cliff side by the force of the ferocious Atlantic seas – demonstrating the might and beauty of nature. The most notable of the sea stacks is located near Yesnaby castle, resembling the Old Man of Hoy (a 450-ft sea stack that is the tallest in the UK), and is at its most dramatic in stormy weather when powerful waves crash around its sides.

THE HIGHLANDS

Usually when we think about 'Scottish' culture we are really thinking about 'Highland' culture. In fact, the things that we typically consider as defining all things Scottish are in abundance in the Highlands: castles, mountains, lochs, glens, clans, heroes, the Gaelic language, Highland Games, ceilidhs, haggis and, of course, the Loch Ness monster. In this chapter be prepared to absorb the beauty of Highland scenery from the bustling city of Inverness to the startling magnificence of Glen Coe

Tarbat Ness

DORNOCH FIRTH, ROSS AND CROMARTY

Tarbat Ness is famed for its lighthouse. Built in 1830 by the famous
Scottish civil engineer, designer and lighthouse builder Robert Stevenson,
it is the third tallest lighthouse in Scotland, reaching 53 m (174 ft) and
is striking in appearance with its two broad red bands. The lighthouse
is located near the fishing village of Portmahomack, which has become
famous itself due to the discovery of the only Pictish monastic settlement
found in Scotland to date in a field south-west of Portmahomack's
former parish church (now the Tarbat Discovery Centre).

River Torridon

WESTER ROSS

The River Torridon in Wester Ross is a small, pretty river that is only
4 miles (6 km) long and which is popular for salmon and trout fishing.
The river flows from Lochan an Iasgair (a small loch) to the outstandingly
beautiful Loch Torridon, with its incredible backdrop of the white
quartzite-tipped, rugged Liathach and Benn Eigh mountains – that rise
around 1000 m (3281 ft) above sea level – and the impressive turreted
mansion house (now a hotel) that decorates its shores.

Suilven

NEAR LOCHINVER, SUTHERLAND

Sometimes called the 'Sugar Loaf', Suilven's name actually derives from the Norse 'Pillar Mountain'. At 728 m (2389 ft) in height Suilven is not among the highest mountains in Scotland, but it is one of the most popular with climbers. Although somewhat daunting because of its unusual shape (like a traditional police officer's helmet from Lochinver and with fierce spiked peaks that dominate the skyline when viewed from the east), the mountain's summit is something of a surprise with gently sloping grassland that belies its rather severe appearance.

Eilean Donan Castle

DORNIE

Eilean Donan Castle has the reputation of being the most Roman castle in Scotland; it certainly is one of the most recognisable and among the most photographed in the country. The castle's setting is particularly dreamlike, situated on a small island of the same name where three lochs (Loch Alsh, Loch Duich and Loch Long) meet. The original thirteenth-century castle was built by King Alexander II (1198–1249), but what remains now is the work of Lieutenant Colonel John MacRae-Gilstrap who rebuilt the castle between 1912 and 1932.

Duncansby Head

NEAR JOHN O'GROATS, CAITHNESS

Duncansby Head is located on the most north-eastern tip of the Scottish mainland. Although it is generally considered that John O'Groats (Duncansby Head's westerly neighbour) is the winner of this accolade, it actually falls short to Duncansby Head by at least a mile or two from Lands End. Nonetheless, Duncansby Head's lack of recognition makes it even more special; without the crowds that head to John O'Groats, this marvellously dramatic work of nature, and the surrounding wildlife, can be truly appreciated without interruption.

Ullapool

LOCH BROOM

Ullapool is a picturesque fishing village that nestles on the shores of Loch Broom. The town's origins go back to 1788 when it was designed and built by Thomas Telford (1757–1834) and the British Fisheries Society. The harbour and the fishing industry has always been the lifeline of the community, sometimes in unexpected ways. For example, during the late 1970s Loch Broom played host to some 60 Russian and East European ships that used the loch from August to January annually to export locally caught mackerel to their native countries.

Urquhart Castle

LOCH NESS

The romantic ruins of Urquhart Castle are situated on a rocky peninsula on the banks of Loch Ness. The castle dates back to around 1230 as it was probably built by the Durward family who had been granted the area in 1229, and survived hundreds of tumultuous years of history, until 1692 when it was blown up to prevent it from becoming a Jacobite stronghold. During the 1930s the castle was bought by a Mr Chewett whose widow donated the castle to the National Trust for Scotland in 2003. The ruin of Urquhart Castle is a popular tourist attraction, and even more so because of the sweeping views over Loch Ness that offer the possibility of a glimpse of Nessie.

Loch Ewe

NEAR COVE, POOLEWE

Pictured above at sunset, the peninsula of Cove glides around one side of the beautiful Loch Ewe. At the centre of the loch is the Isle of Ewe and at its head the lovely village of Poolewe, where the small River Ewe runs from Loch Maree into the sea. Also at this end of the loch is Inverewe Garden, founded by Osgood Mackenzie (1842–1922) in 1862, and considered to be among the finest gardens in Europe. They are affectionately called the 'Oasis of the North' because of the diversity of plants that are able to flourish in the warmer Gulf-Stream climate.

Plockton

NEAR KYLE OF LOCHALSH

Snuggling up to the shore of Loch Carron, Plockton (pictured left) is a picturesque village of pretty cottages that curve around the small harbour. The village was originally a crofting hamlet, until the end of the 1700s, and became a place of refuge for the displaced during the Clearances. In later years Plockton prospered from the fishing industry, although those days are long gone. Nowadays it is a popular tourist spot, particularly for artists because of the quality of light during the summer months – and also because of the village's contrasting qualities, like the palm trees that line the main street in juxtaposition to the rugged heather-speckled landscape.

Loch Poulary

GLEN GARRY

Situated within Glen Garry is the large fresh water Loch Garry, which from above forms the shape of a mini-Scotland. Between Loch Garry and Loch Quoich is a small expansion of water formed off the River Garry – this is Loch Poulary. At only 2 miles (3 km) long, Loch Poulary was created during the damming of the River Garry as part of the Garry-Moriston Hydro-Electric Scheme. Although not the most romantic of origins, the loch fits seamlessly into the rugged Highland landscape, and to fishermen this little loch is the 'jewel in the crown' with its plentiful supply of freshwater trout and salmon.

Mallaig

LOCHABER

Once Europe's busiest herring port, Mallaig continues to be at the centre of the Scottish fishing industry, with their biggest income sourced from the large catches of prawns and seafood. The busy working port also operates the many ferry services that run to Skye, the Small Isles and the Knoydart peninsula. The terminus of the West Highland Railway journey from Fort William is also in Mallaig as well as the final station of the spectacular steam-powered *Jacobite*, which is perhaps the best and most scenic train journey in the world.

Inverness

Inverness is the only city in the Highlands – it was granted city status by the Queen in December 2000 – and is the unofficial Capital of the Highlands, a long way from its origins as an ancient fort. Situated at the north end of the Great Glen, where the River Ness flows into the Moray Firth, it has a bustling but small, modern city centre. The heart of the city is its river, River Ness, with focal points like Inverness Castle, the cathedral and Eden Court theatre blending history with modernity.

Five Sisters of Kintail

GLEN SHIEL

The mountains that rise above Glen Shiel are affectionately known as the Five Sisters of Kintail. According to legend, two Irish princes were washed ashore on the banks of Loch Duich and fell in love with two of the King of Kintail's daughters. The princes returned to Ireland with the princesses as their brides and promised the king that they would send their five brothers to wed the king's five remaining daughters. The king's daughters waited all their life for their suitors to return and in desperation begged the Grey Magician of Coire Dhunnaid for immortality, whereupon the magician turned them into mountains.

Corpach and Ben Nevis

NEAR FORT WILLIAM

One of the best views of Ben Nevis is from the village of Corpach (as pictured on the previous pages) as the mountain soars sinisterly above Fort William. Ben Nevis reaches 1344 m (4406 ft) at its peak and is Scotland's highest mountain. The challenges of the mountain make it perhaps the most popular mountain in Scotland to climb, with tens of thousands of climbers trying to reach its summit every year. Unfortunately, with changeable weather conditions the mountain can also be the most dangerous, with climbers often lifted or carried off to safety.

Glen Coe

'Glen Coe' is thought to mean 'narrow glen' as well as the more poignant – considering its history – 'glen of weeping'. Glen Coe is one of the most striking and majestic places in Scotland where the narrow glen is loomed over by wild, enveloping mountains. It is not only famous for its topography, however. On 13 February 1692 at 5 am, the abhorrent Massacre of Glen Coe took place, where 38 MacDonalds from the Clan MacDonald of Glencoe were killed as well as another 40 women and children who consequently died after their homes were burned down.

Glenfinnan Monument

LOCH SHIEL

On 19 August 1745 at the north end of Loch Shiel, Bonnie Prince
Charlie (1720–88) raised his standard to fight for the exiled Stuarts to
return to the throne. Although Bonnie Prince Charlie and his men got
as far as Derby, on the 16 April 1746 their mission ended in bloody
failure at Culloden, and the typical way of Highland life was brutally
exterminated. In 1815 the Glenfinnan Monument, designed by James
Gillespie Graham (1776–1855), was erected to commemorate the
clansmen who fought and died in honour of the Stuarts.

Rannoch Moor
LOCHABER AND PERTH AND KINROSS

Considered to be one of the last truly wild places remaining in Scotland, Rannoch Moor in rainy weather conditions can sometimes have an almost other-worldly, desolate appearance. Indeed, Robert Louis Stevenson (1850–94) described it in his novel *Kidnapped* as 'A wearier looking desert a man never saw'. Created 20,000 years ago by glacier movement, the moor spans 12,800 acres and is an upland plateau scattered with numerous lochs, lochans, peat bogs and streams. It is surrounded by mountains, some reaching over 914 m (3000 ft).

Eas Chia-aig Falls
NEAR CLUNES, LOCH LOCHY

At the head of Loch Lochy and to the left of Clunes is a darkly wooded and mossy twisting pass that leads through the hills, romantically named Mile Dorcha (meaning 'dark mile'). The gift at the other end when entering into the daylight is the spectacular Eas Chai-aig Falls, where the frothy water cascades down the side of the valley. A stone staircase leads to the top of the falls, and the views from here are even better. The spot also featured in the film *Rob Roy* (1995).

GRAMPIAN AND ABERDEEN

The Grampian Highlands deserve the reputation they
have earned as Scotland's 'castle country' with more
than 70 castles in this area as well as a multitude of
stone circles, standing stones and hill forts that all have
their own histories. The region also houses more than
half of Scotland's malt whisky distilleries. The undisputed
capital city of the region is Aberdeen – with its
reputation as the 'granite city', it truly shines. Stunning
photographs and accompanying text bring to life
Aberdeen's Union Street, the ruins of the beautiful
medieval Elgin Cathedral and the area's main river the
River Dee, to mention only a few.

Union Street

ABERDEEN

The Granite City, Aberdeen, is often referred to as the oil capital of Europe and is indeed one of the most prosperous cities in Scotland. Aberdeen's main streets with their austere buildings are impressive, and none more so than Union Street (pictured above). Built between 1801 and 1805, Union Street was named after the 1800 Act of Union with Ireland and, at almost a mile long, it is home to some of Aberdeen's most revered granite buildings, such as the Town and County Bank, the Music hall, the Palace Hotel and the National Bank of Scotland.

Aberdeen Harbour

ABERDEEN

Aberdeen Harbour, pictured here (left), with the city centre beyond, is the principal port in northern Scotland, handling around five million tonnes of cargo annually. One of the busiest Trust ports in the UK, it works as a port for cruise ships, international cargo, the offshore oil and gas industries, and the fishing industry. The Northlink Ferries service also operates from the harbour offering services to Kirkwall and the Shetland Islands. A little further east, in Hong Kong, there is another Aberdeen Harbour, apparently named so by some home-sick ex-pat Aberdonians.

Crathes Castle

ABERDEENSHIRE

Crathes Castle (owned by the National Trust for Scotland) is one of the best-loved castles in Scotland. A fairytale-like design with a pink-tinted exterior of turrets and corbelling, it has an interior that is equally as impressive. Almost like stepping back in time, the fine tapestries, painted ceilings and grand rooms, like the Laird's Bedroom, impart a sense of the history of the Burnett family, who lived here over the centuries. The castle gardens are also awe-inspiring and almost as famous as the castle itself.

Dunnottar Castle

NEAR STONEHAVEN, ABERDEENSHIRE

A ruined medieval fortress, Dunnottar Castle dates back to the late 400s when it served as a Pictish fort. Famous visitors include William Wallace (c. 1270–1305), Mary Queen of Scots (1542–87) and the Marquis of Montrose. The castle is most famous for its involvement in saving the Scottish Crown Jewels, the 'Honours of Scotland', from the hands of Oliver Cromwell (1599–1658) in 1652. The jewels were lowered down the 50 m (164 ft) cliffs to a local woman pretending to collect seaweed and were buried in the parish church near Kinneff, so when Cromwell's men raided the castle, they were nowhere to be found.

River Dee

NEAR BRAEMAR, ABERDEENSHIRE

Stretching for 90 miles (140 km), the River Dee rises high in the heart of the Cairngorm mountains on the plateau of Braeriach, which is the highest source of any major river in the UK at approximately 1219 m (4000 ft) above sea level, and flows through Royal Deeside, reaching the North Sea at Aberdeen. Also referred to as the 'Silver Dee', it is a tumbling, crystal water river, plentiful in salmon, that winds its way through the beautiful surrounding countryside of Braemar (pictured here), Invercauld, Balmoral and Ballater.

Castle Fraser

NEAR ABERDEEN

The grand, baronial Castle Fraser is the most elaborate of the Scottish castles built in the Z plan design with an array of turrets, balustrades and gables combined to dramatic effect. Work began on the castle in 1575 by the 6th laird, Michael Fraser, and was completed in 1636. Portraiture of the Fraser family can be found around the castle, including a family portrait by Raeburn (1756–1823). The acres of woodland that surround the garden are idyllic, to which the majestic castle forms the perfect backdrop.

Stonehaven

ABERDEENSHIRE

Stonehaven is situated 15 miles (24 km) south from Aberdeen and has benefited from the rewards of the oil wealth mostly associated with its larger neighbour. Fishing and tourism are the town's biggest industries, with the nearby Dunnottar Castle (see p.51) attracting the crowds. Of particular interest in Stonehaven is the charismatic and charming Old Town and harbour. By the harbour is The Ship Inn, built in 1771, and the Tolbooth, a small museum of local interest, which was partly built by Robert Louis Stevenson's grandfather.

Pennan

ABERDEENSHIRE

Pennan (pictured above in the distance) is famous for being the
location of the film *Local Hero* (1983), the iconic red phone box on the
quayside, facing the Pennan Inn, being a favourite tourist attraction. A
sleepy little place, it consists of only one street of white cottages that
squeeze in where the cliffs end and the sea begins. The little harbour,
situated at the east end of the village, is dotted with a few fishing boats
but is mostly used for leisure pursuits.

Craigievar Castle

NEAR BALLATER

Built in the early seventeenth century by the wealthy Aberdonian
merchant William Forbes (1739–1806), Craigievar Castle is a six-storey
baronial masterpiece of turrets, cupolas and corbelling. The Forbes family
lived there for over three centuries and entertained high-profile guests
such as Queen Victoria (1819–1901) and Prince Albert (1819–61), who
were drawn by the beauty of the castle and the charm of its Jacobean
interior. The castle, and its surrounding acreage, is now maintained by the
National Trust for Scotland, to whom it was given in 1963.

Covesea Lighthouse

LOSSIEMOUTH, MORAY

Covesea Lighthouse is a 5 m (18 ft) white, conical tower and was built in 1844 by Alan Stevenson (1807–65). Although now fully automated, it once worked using a clockwork mechanism and by the skill of its keeper. The lighthouse is situated on the largest of the Covesea Skerries, a series of little islands and rocks off the Moray Coast that submerge in water at high tide. The town of Lossiemouth with its championship golf course lies 3 miles (5 km) to the west of the lighthouse.

Bow Fiddle Rock

PORTNOCKIE, MORAY

Bow Fiddle Rock, so-called owing to its arch resembling a violin bow, is a stunning natural arch made of quartzite rocks that have been cut away by the power of the sea. It is the village of Portnockie's most visited tourist attraction and is home to a myriad of sea-bird life such as gulls and cormorants. In early summer it is possible to see Eider Ducks swimming around the rock and less commonly grey seals will haul up on the shoreline. The cliff-top plateau has views as far as Troop Head near Fraserburgh.

Elgin Cathedral

ELGIN, MORAY

One of the most magnificent ruins in Scotland, Elgin Cathedral dates
back to the 1200s and signs of the cathedral's former glory are evident
all over the site. One can only imagine how powerful a building of such
size and stature appeared to its congregation. The west front of the
cathedral is architecturally awe-inspiring with two massive towers that
frame the processional doorway, still bidding worshippers (or more likely
nowadays visitors) to enter. There are steps that lead to the top of the
north tower, offering lovely views across Elgin.

Findochty

MORAY

A typically Scottish little village, Findochty's origins date back to the early
1400s. The focus of the village is its harbour, known as Crooked Haven,
with a series of pretty cottages that follow its curve. Not much fishing
is done from the harbour these days and the water is used more for
leisurely sailing. No hoards of tourists are to be found in Findochty,
but the village's authenticity and truly Scottish charm make it somewhere
to be treasured.

CENTRAL SCOTLAND

Often regarded as the 'heart of Scotland', Central
Scotland has an incredibly varied landscape, the most
famous of which is probably the stunning Loch Lomond.
At the centre of the region is Stirling, the beating heart
of Scottish history with its famous castle. To the north is
Loch Katrine and the Trossachs – Rob Roy country –
with its superb loch and mountain scenery. Flick through
the following pages of this chapter to discover more…

Queen's View

LOCH TUMMEL, PERTH AND KINROSS

Queen's View is among the most famous and most scenic spots in Scotland. Most probably named after Queen Victoria, though some argue it is also named after Mary Queen of Scots – they were both admirers of this sweeping landscape. The beauty of Queen's View alone makes it worthy of the regal title. Situated just outside Pitlochry, Queen's view is a breathtaking panorama of the clear waters of Loch Tummel and the surrounding mountain scenery, which on a clear day stretches as far as Glen Coe.

Kenmore

NEAR ABERFELDY, PERTH AND KINROSS

Idyllically situated on an outlet at the eastern end of Loch Tay, Kenmore is a beautiful village of white-washed cottages. Most unique is the village's main street, which features a lovely clock tower at one end and boasts the nineteenth-century Taymouth Castle, built by the Campbells of Glenorchy (now used as a golf club), at the other. Kenmore is also home to Scotland's oldest inn dating back to 1572, and a poem written on the wall by Robert Burns in 1787 certainly verifies its authenticity.

Scone Palace

PERTH AND KINROSS

Home of the Earl and Countess of Mansfield, Scone Palace is steeped in history. Having been the seat of parliaments and the crowning place of Scottish kings, it was also the home of the Stone of Destiny from the ninth century until 1296 when it was moved to Westminster Abbey by Edward I, as well as being the legendary setting for William Shakespeare's (1564–1616) *Macbeth*. The palace that stands today, however, was actually only built in 1802 by the English architect William Atkinson who then went on to build Abbotsford House (*see* p.127) for Sir Walter Scott (1771–1832).

Falls of Dochart

KILLIN, STIRLING

One of the most scenic and most photographed sections of the River Dochart is where the spectacular rapids of the Falls of Dochart rush under the bridge leading into the village of Killin, at the western end of Loch Tay. From the bridge, there is a magnificent view of the falls as they cascade around the island of Inchbuie (or Innes Buie), the burial ground of the clan MacNab who lived in Glen Dochart and Strath Fillan for 800 years.

Loch Ard, Aberfoyle

THE TROSSACHS, STIRLING

Loch Ard (pictured on the previous pages) in the Trossachs lies 3 miles (5 km) west of the village of Aberfoyle and to the east of Loch Lomond. The loch is famously described by Sir Walter Scott in his novel *Rob Roy* (1818) as 'an enchanting sheet of water'. Rob Roy's cave is also located on Loch Ard, where the man himself formulated many of his plans as an outlaw. On the south shore is a ruined castle, built by Murdoch Stewart (c. 1362–1425), Duke of Albany, Regent of Scotland.

Old Stirling Bridge and Wallace Monument

STIRLING

Sir William Wallace is one of the most well-known and best-loved Scottish figures around the world, especially since the release of *Braveheart* (1995). The Battle of Stirling Bridge took place on 11 September 1297 on the original wooden bridge, which lay further upstream from the remaining Old Stirling Bridge (pictured here with the Wallace Monument in the background). Wallace and his men descended from higher ground and attacked the English as they assembled on the bridge, winning one of the most monumental battles in Scottish history. Scottish casualties were light, but the loss of Wallace's faithful friend and joint general, Sir Andrew Moray, was a great loss to the Scottish side.

Stirling Castle

STIRLING

Stirling Castle stands proud on crags of volcanic rock and is one of the most important castles in Scottish history. In terms of the castle's location (it can be seen from miles around in every direction) it even gives Edinburgh Castle a run for its money. The plains below the castle (pictured here) were where some of Scotland's most important and decisive battles took place. Within the castle grounds of particular interest are the gatehouse, Great Hall and the Renaissance Royal Palace. The castle is now cared for by Historic Scotland.

Loch Lomond

ARGYLL AND BUTE

Loch Lomond is the largest fresh water loch in the UK at 24 miles
(39 km) long, 5 miles (8 km) wide and at its deepest 183 m (600 ft)
deep. Loch Lomond is also one of the most written (and sung) about
locations in the world; the old Scots song 'Bonnie Banks O' Loch
Lomond (You Take the High Road)' perhaps being the most famous.
Loch Lomond contains 38 islands, some of which are inhabited, and
the area is renowned for its natural beauty, which features both
lowland and highland characteristics.

City Square

DUNDEE CITY CENTRE, DUNDEE

Dundee is the fourth largest city in Scotland and is regarded as the
'City of Discovery' because of the city's scientific heritage, in particular
the RRS *Discovery*, which was built in Dundee to sail Robert Falcon
Scott (1868–1832) to the Antarctic. Dundee's City Square (pictured
here illuminated in the evening) lies at the heart of the city centre and is
home to Dundee City Chambers and the impressive Doric-columned
Caird Hall, which plays host to the city's graduation ceremonies as well
as various concerts, plays and exhibitions throughout the year.

Loch Katrine

THE TROSSACHS

Loch Katrine's name is believed to derive from the highland *caterans* who used to steal cattle, and whatever else they could, from the lowlands, bringing it back to the Trossachs where they could hide their booty and seek shelter around the glens and lochs. The tourist industry began to surge in the Trossachs with the release of Sir Walter Scott's first major work *The Lady of the Lake* (1810), to which the scenery and the landscape around Loch Katrine was the author's inspiration. It is fitting that the steamship, aptly named *Sir Walter Scott* (pictured here) has been taking visitors around the loch for over a century.

The Falkirk Wheel

FALKIRK

The Falkirk Wheel is the world's first and only rotating boat lift, and was opened by the Queen in May 2002. A magnificent and beautiful functional structure, it is a feat of twenty-first-century engineering, and is the centrepiece of the Millennium Link (a huge canal restoration project that resulted in connecting the Union Canal with the Forth and Clyde Canal). The Falkirk Wheel is also a hugely popular tourist attraction. Many are happy just to soak up the sheer glory of the 35 m (115 ft) structure, but for the more adventurous the 'Wheel Experience' allows you to ride through the tunnel and on the wheel itself.

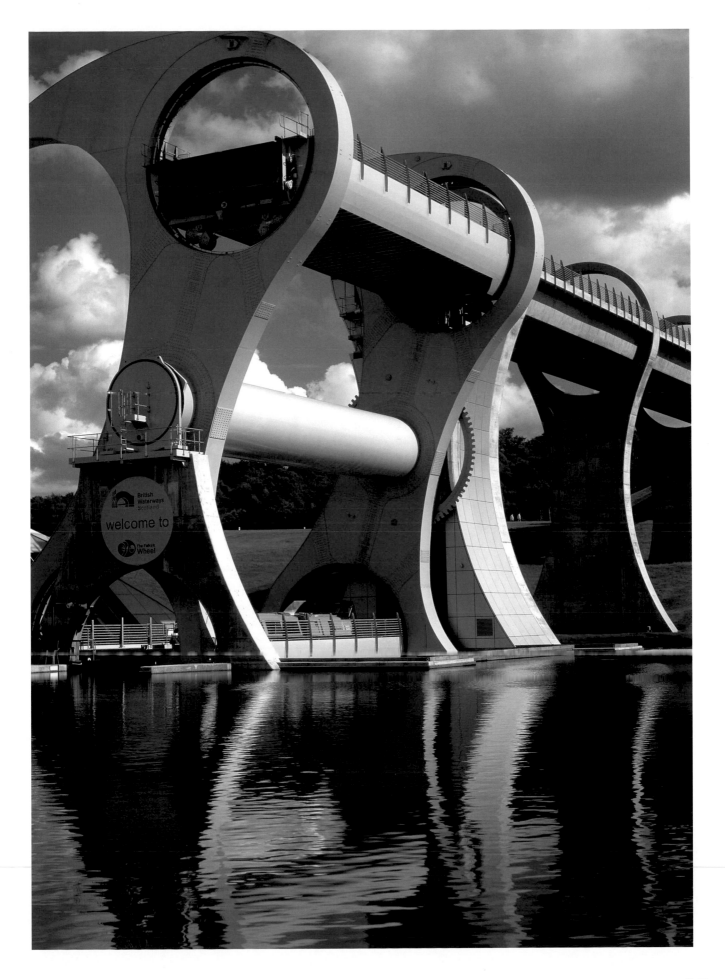

The Falkirk Wheel
welcome to
British Waterways Scotland

EDINBURGH, LOTHIAN AND FIFE

What is there to say when in this chapter lies the most
famous of all castles, Edinburgh Castle, the architectural
wonder that is the Forth Rail Bridge and one of the
most prestigious university and golfing towns in
the country, St Andrews. In this chapter you can
wander down Edinburgh's Royal Mile, imagine the
city's military tattoo or learn about life in days
gone by in Preston Mill, East Lothian.

Forth Rail Bridge

NEAR EDINBURGH, LOTHIAN

The more famous of the Forth bridges, the Forth Rail Bridge is possibly the finest bridge in Britain and is recognised all over the world. Designed by Sir Benjamin Baker (1840–1907) and Sir John Fowler (1817–98), it was built with a hefty price tag of £2½ million. The massive structure is strengthened with three cantilever towers and rises to 110 m (360 ft) above water at its highest points. Construction of the bridge took seven years, opening for use on 4 March 1890 – the Prince of Wales (later King Edward VII 1841–1910) presided over the ceremony.

Edinburgh Military Tattoo

EDINBURGH

A huge success with locals and international tourists alike, the Military Tattoo commands an audience of approximately 217,000 each year and boasts performances from over 30 countries worldwide. The evening begins with the phenomenal marching of Scottish soldiers across the drawbridge to the Esplanade, booming out tunes such as 'The Skye Boat Song' and 'The Garb of Old Gaul'. Throughout the evening, home-grown talent and international guests enthral the audience. The night is rounded off with spectacular fireworks and a skin-tingling recital of 'Auld Lang Syne'.

The Palace of Holyroodhouse

EDINBURGH

The Palace of Holyroodhouse is the official residence of Her Majesty the Queen in Scotland. At the edge of Holyrood Park, it is located at the eastern end of the Royal Mile, descending from Edinburgh Castle. Little of the original building remains today: the palace was seriously damaged by the invasion of the Earl of Hertford in 1544 and, later, by Cromwell in 1650. The building that we recognise is credited to the reconstruction of the palace, which was undertaken by architect Sir William Bruce (1630–1710) and builder Robert Mylne (1633–1710) for Charles II in 1671.

Scottish Parliament Building (Office Window)

EDINBURGH

Swathed in controversy, the subject of the Scottish Parliament building is never short of debate – whether it is on the streets of Scotland or in the Debating Chamber itself. This is hardly surprising, when the building came at a cost of £431 million, instead of the original estimate of £50 million. Nonetheless, the striking Enric Miralles (1955–2000) building signifies the rebirth of a nation. As the Queen said in her speech on the official opening of the parliament on 9 October 2004, it is 'a landmark of twenty-first-century democracy'.

The Scott Monument

EDINBURGH

This Gothic monument in Princes Street Gardens rises to 67 m (200 ft) and was built in 1846 in commemoration of Edinburgh's literary son, Sir Walter Scott. Designed by George Meikle Kemp (1795–1844), a self-taught architect who won the project in a competition, the design of the monument is very much influenced by Melrose Abbey. Inside the blackened sandstone structure are 287 steps to the top, where the views of the Edinburgh skyline are stunning. A statue of Scott, by Sir John Steell (1804–91), is to be found below the arches of the monument.

Edinburgh Castle

EDINBURGH

Rising from an ancient volcanic plug, Edinburgh Castle looms over the capital city from a height of 80 m (262 ft). A majestic sight to behold, it is the city's biggest tourist attraction; it dominates the skyline just as much as it has Edinburgh's extensive and complex history. The variety of architectural styles demonstrate both the castle's history and service as a stronghold and seat of kings. Housed in the castle is the famous Stone of Destiny, seized by the English and taken to Westminster Abbey in 1296, and only returned to Scotland in 1996.

John Knox's House

EDINBURGH

This fifteenth-century house has remained largely unaltered since the 1550s when the Mosman family, who were goldsmiths to Mary Queen of Scots, lived there. It rises to three storeys and is the most picturesque building on the High Street. Outside it features a sundial of Moses pointing to the sun, a water well and a set of forestairs. Many doubt that the famous Protestant reformer John Knox (c. 1514–72) ever lived there, but, if he did, it would have been between 1561 and 1572. The interior of the house is highly decorated and has some fine hand-painted ceilings. The house is now run by the Church of Scotland and functions as a museum, where relics of Knox and the Reformation are exhibited.

Near Cupar

FIFE

This landscape, located close to the historic town of Cupar, is alive with colour. Miles of bright yellow fields, most probably rapeseed fields, which are common all over Scotland, liven up the traditional landscape. In Cupar itself there are a fine collection of historic churches as well as the beautiful River Eden and Park.

Elie

FIFE

Elie is a lovely seaside resort that has been popular with families since Victorian times when the village became accessible by steamer and train. The village merges into the village of Earlsferry, half a mile along the bay of the harbour, and together they are a big attraction with the yachting and golfing crowds. The villages' oldest buildings are located on South Street, where there is Earlsferry's town hall and Elie's local shops. On High Street, Elie's parish church, with its unusual clock tower, dates back to 1639.

St Andrews (Cathedral Ruins)

FIFE

To say that St Andrews has a lot going for it is an understatement. The town really does deserve its fame. With its world-renowned golf course, perhaps the best university in the country (from which its most recent famous graduate is Prince William), St Andrews Castle and its stunning medieval architecture and Victorian streets, what else could you ask for. Of the ruins at St Andrews Cathedral (pictured), what remains is quite fragmented, but the nave and west gable are best preserved. The town's traditional harbour and the adjoining beach, East Sands, are where locals and visitors go to take a break.

Crail

FIFE

Situated 10 miles (16 km) south east of St Andrews, Crail inhabits the mostly easterly coastal settlement along the south side of the East Neuk of Fife, giving the place a real feeling of seclusion. Crail has been a bustling community since the 1100s, and King Robert the Bruce authorised it as a royal burgh in 1310. It is one of Scotland's most photographed villages. The beautiful harbour, pictured here, is usually dotted with colourful fishing boats and showcases the pretty white-fronted houses with grey slate or red-tiled roofs.

Preston Mill

EAST LOTHIAN

The picturesque eighteenth-century Preston Mill sits at the edge of the River Tyne, powering its water wheel and grain milling machinery. The conical roofed kiln and red pantile roofed buildings, and the nearby mill pond graced with ducks and geese, creates an idyll that is irresistible to the artists and photographers who gather here regularly for inspiration. The mill has not produced grain commercially since 1959, but there is an exhibition on milling, and just watching and listening to the noise of the machinery in action transports you back to bygone days when the miller was at work.

GLASGOW, CLYDE VALLEY AND ARGYLL

Scotland's biggest city, and according to some its best,
Glasgow is illustrated beautifully here, with stunning
photography of the Kelvingrove Art Gallery and Museum,
Glasgow University and the changing face of the River
Clyde. Alongside these cityscapes you'll find the likes of
the incredible Mount Stuart on the Isle of Bute, the
bustling harbour of Oban, and the pretty fishing village
of Tarbert. Read on to discover more…

River Clyde

GLASGOW

Historically known as the 'second city of the empire', Glasgow has always relied on its river. From the late nineteenth century the development of the heavy industries, particularly engineering and shipbuilding, meant that the River Clyde was a hive of activity. By the 1960s and 1970s, however, many of the shipyards began to close down. The city mourned its loss as the Clyde had always been in the Glaswegians' veins, and its future seemed bleak. Nowadays, the Clydeside in Glasgow city centre is home to the financial district, bringing big business to the city and a massive economic boost. Alongside the River Clyde these days, prestigious new flats snuggle up to the medieval Glasgow cathedral (pictured).

Glasgow University from Kelvingrove Park

GLASGOW

The spire of Glasgow University can be seen from many vantage points around the city and is a reminder of the city's academic heritage. A few of the names it can boast to have educated include Lord Kelvin (1824–1907), Adam Smith (c. 1723–90) and John Logie Baird (1888–1946) to modern day success stories such as the late Donald Dewar (1937–2000), Menzies Campbell (b.1941) and Charles Kennedy (b.1959). Situated in the city's west-end, the area is one of the city's quirkiest and well-heeled areas: a mixture of student informality and über-poshness. A big draw is also Kelvingrove Park and its gallery (see p.95).

George Square

GLASGOW

George Square lies in the heart of Glasgow's centre and at its head is the city's famous and architecturally stunning City Chambers (built in 1888). Once Glasgow Square used to be a picturesque grassy square, but for some reason Glasgow City Council decided to fill it in with concrete in the early 1990s. Still the square does have pretty flowerbeds and its benches provide workers, shoppers and tourists some respite from the busy city centre. George Square is also the venue for Glasgow's main party at Hogmany (New Year's Eve) and sometimes plays host to small concerts throughout the year.

Kelvingrove Art Gallery and Museum

GLASGOW

Kelvingrove Art Gallery and Museum is the biggest and the best of Glasgow's galleries and one of the city's most definable and attractive landmarks – even though it was built the wrong way round from its original design. The gallery has undergone a massive renovation project and has increased its content by 50 per cent. Among the most notable artists featured are Rembrandt, Titian and Dalí (*St John of the Cross*) who mingle in nicely with the native talent such as the Glasgow Boys and the Scottish Colourists.

Oban

ARGYLL AND BUTE

Translating from Scottish Gaelic as 'little bay', Oban is now a very busy port, ferrying thousands of visitors annually to Mull, Colonsay, Coll, Tiree, Lismore, and Barra and South Uist in the Western Isles – it is no coincidence that it is regarded as the 'Gateway to the Highlands'. Oban is much more than just a stopover when travelling further afield. It has been a popular holiday destination since Victorian times. Indeed, Queen Victoria herself regarded the place as 'one of the finest places we've seen'.

Castle Stalker

APPIN, LOCH LINNHE, ARGYLL AND BUTE

Castle Stalker is a four-storey tower house (built in 1540) and is one of the finest and best preserved medieval castles in western Scotland. Located 1.5 miles (2 km) north east of Port Appin in an islet at the mouth of Loch Laich (by Loch Linnhe), it is particularly picturesque and much photographed. The castle was abandoned in 1870 and was left to deteriorate. Lieutenant Colonel Stewart Allward restored it from its ruinous condition in the late 1960s, and the property is still owned by his family.

Tarbert

ARGYLL AND BUTE

There are a few Tarberts in Scotland, each one a narrow piece of land where two lochs almost meet. In this case the two lochs are West Loch Kintyre and East Loch Tarbert, around which Tarbert's harbour is built. An attractive fishing village it has become very popular with the yachting crowd, and their yachts, as well as pretty fishing boats, decorate the harbour. On the hillside above the harbour are the ruins of Robert the Bruce's castle (later captured by James IV), which dates back to the year 1200.

Mount Stuart

ISLE OF BUTE, ARGYLL AND BUTE

The magnificent Victorian Gothic Mount Stuart was the vision of the 3rd Marquess of Bute, a direct descendant of Robert the Bruce, and the Scottish architect Robert Rowand Anderson. Old Mount Stuart had been destroyed by fire in 1877 and both men made visionary designs for its replacement, the Mount Stuart we witness today. Ironically, their vision was never fully completed, but the late 6th Marquess set about restoring the property in the 1980s, a project that is still ongoing. The doors of Mount Stuart opened to the public in 1995.

Kilchurn Castle

LOCH AWE, ARGYLL AND BUTE

The substantial ruin of Kilchurn Castle (pictured on previous pages) that remains today began as a five-storey tower house, built by Sir Colin Campbell, first Lord of Glenorchy, in 1450 with further buildings added during the 1500s and 1600s. A treacherous storm seriously damaged the castle in 1760, and the upturned turret of a tower still survives in the centre of the castle's courtyard. Located on a small island in Loch Awe, a steamer sails out to the castle from Loch Awe Pier. The property is managed by Historic Scotland.

Dunoon

ARGYLL AND BUTE

In the west of Scotland you'll often hear locals comment that 'Dunoon, Dunoon is a bonnie wee toon'. And that's because Dunoon was a place of escape for many looking for a holiday away from the city, Glasgow in particular. Wealthy Glaswegians bought villas in the town, but for the masses it was a hugely popular tourist destination. By 1820, the pier (pictured here) had been built, and the ferry from the River Clyde arrived there regularly, with both steamer and train services up and running by 1890.

Glen Orchy

ARGYLL AND BUTE

Stretching for 12 miles (19 km), Glen Orchy is a stunning valley covered with conifer trees where the River Orchy (pictured here) flows south-westerly between Bridge of Orchy and Dalmally. With only a population of ten, the majority of people who visit the glen are either tourists, anglers, walkers or artists, attracted by the peaceful location and the beauty of the natural environment. A famous son of the Glen is Duncan Bàn MacIntyre (1724–1812) who is best known for his poem about Ben Doran titled 'Moladh Beinn Dobhrainn'.

Inveraray Castle
ARGYLL AND BUTE

A mix of Baroque, Palladian and Gothic styles with four French-inspired conical spires pointing out from castellated towers, Inveraray Castle was the first of its kind in Scotland. Designed at various stages by Sir John Vanbrugh (1664–1726), Roger Morris and William Adam (1689–1748) (Scotland's most revered architect), work began on the castle in 1746 and saw completion in 1789. The castle is home to the chief of the Campbell clan, the Duke of Argyll. Many portraits of the Campbell's ancestors throughout the centuries are on display throughout the castle.

Duart Castle
ISLE OF MULL, ARGYLL AND BUTE

The original Duart Castle dates from the thirteenth century, and is believed to have been built for the MacDougalls. The present castle has been the ancestral home of the Clan Maclean from the late fourteenth century to the present day. Although a family home, parts of the castle are open to the public, including the Banqueting Hall, the Sea Room, various state rooms and the dungeons. Among the extensive castle grounds is the Millennium Wood, which features many of the trees and shrubs that are indigenous to the area.

Rothesay

A popular holiday destination, Rothesay (whose harbour is pictured here) is the main town on the Isle of Bute, which lies in the Firth of Clyde across the water from the seaside town of Largs in North Ayrshire. Rothesay is home to one of the best surviving medieval castles in Scotland, Rothesay Castle, and it used to be the seat of the Marquises of Bute before Mount Stuart (see p.99). Outside of Rothesay, the landscape of the Isle of Bute is mostly rural. On the south of the island the other main tourist attraction is the ruins of St Blane's Chapel.

SOUTHWEST SCOTLAND AND THE BORDERS

Heading south along the west coast is 'Burns Country',
that is Ayrshire, and here you will find the Brig O'Doon,
featured in Burns' poem 'Tam O'Shanter', and the
stunning Culzean Castle and Country Park. Cross the
water over to the Isle of Arran, known as 'Scotland in
miniature' or try and catch a glance of the Ailsa Craig,
better known as 'Paddy's Milestone'. As you reach
the borders, you'll be mesmerised by the area's
resplendent castles and the famous four abbeys.
The journey starts here...

Isle of Whithorn Harbour

Known simply as 'the isle', the Isle of Whithorn has not actually been an island since 1790 when the causeway that connects the village to the mainland was built. The harbour has always been the main focal point of the village and in days gone by it was where the necessities of village life arrived in cargoes full of coal, fertiliser and timber. It was here that the *Countess of Galloway* docked, taking passengers to Liverpool and those emigrating to the New World or Australia. Nowadays the fishing boats in the harbour make their living from the locally fresh caught water crabs and lobsters.

Mull of Galloway

The Mull of Galloway is Scotland's most southerly point and one the country's least known areas. With a landscape that resembles that of the north of Scotland, it is hard to believe that Skiddaw in the English Lake District is only 68 miles (109 km) away. The dramatic cliffs (pictured here) rise to 76 m (250 ft) above sea level and on top there is an attractive lighthouse, which was built in 1830 by Robert Stevenson, and a visitor centre. The Mull of Galloway has an unspoilt beauty and air of tranquillity.

Sweetheart Abbey

NEAR DUMFRIES, DUMFRIES AND GALLOWAY

The remains of Sweetheart Abbey are located near the village of New Abbey, south of Dumfries. Set against the backdrop of the rolling hills that climb to the summit of Criffel, the abbey's history is as romantic as its location. Founded by Lady Devorgilla of Galloway in 1273, the abbey was built in memory of her late husband, John Balliol. At her own request, after her death in 1289, Lady Devorgilla was buried in the sanctuary of the abbey church with her husband's embalmed heart beside her. The monks of the abbey named it 'Sweetheart' or *Dulce Cor* in her memory.

Portpatrick

NEAR STRANRAER, DUMFRIES AND GALLOWAY

Portpatrick's location is a bit unusual in that it is almost the most western place in Southern Scotland and is almost the most southern place in Western Scotland. A traditional harbour town, Portpatrick looks over the Irish Channel to Donaghdee. The heart of the port has always been its harbour, and in summer months it is brightened with the colour and variety of its boats. One of the best views of the village is from the harbour wall, where the entirety of the village and the inner harbour can be appreciated.

Drumlanrig Castle

DUMFRIES AND GALLOWAY

Completed in 1691 by William Douglas (1637–95), 1st Duke of
Queensberry, Drumlanrig Castle is one of the finest grand Renaissance
palaces in Southern Scotland. Surrounded by the massive 120,000 acre
Queensberry Estate, country park and Victorian gardens, the grandeur
is unquestionable. However, the allure of such aristocracy coincides
with the endless recreational possibilities that are on offer on the
estate: fishing, shooting, country walks, cycle paths and mountain
biking to name but a few.

Ailsa Craig

NEAR GIRVAN, AYRSHIRE

Affectionately known as 'Paddy's Milestone', because of its location in
the sea half-way between Glasgow and Belfast, Ailsa Craig is a small
island that lies a mere ten miles (16 km) from mainland Girvan.
Formed from the rock of the root of an extinct volcano, it rises to
340 m (1,114 ft). Famously the granite from Ailsa Craig is used to
make curling balls, which are used by the Scottish team in the Winter
Olympics. The island is also a bird sanctuary.

Brig O'Doon
ALLOWAY, AYRSHIRE

Now, do thy speedy utmost, Meg,
And win the key-stone of the brig;
There, at them thou thy tail may toss,
A running stream they dare na cross!

(Extract from 'Tam O'Shanter', by Robert Burns)

The Brig O'Doon is the bridge that Burns describes in the climax of the poem 'Tam O'Shanter' (see above). Situated in an idyllic spot the small, arched Brig O'Doon crosses the waters of the River Doon and is a favourite landscape for artists. One of the best paintings is by David Roberts and it is on display at the Burns Cottage Museum.

Culzean Castle

AYRSHIRE

Robert Adam's final masterpiece, the eighteenth-century Culzean Castle was built for David Kennedy, the 10th Earl of Cassillis. Perched above the cliff side of the Firth of Forth, with views across to the Isle of Arran, Culzean is one of the best-loved and finest Georgian castles in the country. Also much loved is its 500-acre country park complete with wooded walks, the Swan Pond, Walled Garden and Adventure Playground. Culzean Castle and Country Park have been cared for by the National Trust for Scotland since 1945.

Goatfell

ISLE OF ARRAN

Often described as 'Scotland in Miniature' because it has so much to offer on one tiny island (20 miles (32 km) long by 10 miles (16 km) wide), the Isle of Arran is a spectacular place and is home to prehistoric remains, stone circles, Brodick castle, pretty harbours and stunning waterfalls. The first port of call for visitors when they arrive is Brodick, nestling underneath the magnificent Goatfell (pictured), which rises to 880 m (2886 ft) at its summit, just falling short of making it a Munro.

Thirlestane Castle

LAUDER, BORDERS

Dating back to the thirteenth century, Thirlestane Castle has been remodelled several times over the years, in the sixteenth, seventeenth and eighteenth centuries, to create what remains today: a beautiful red sandstone, splendid turreted castle that is a mixture of the Scottish baronial style with touches of the Renaissance. The Maitland family home since 1590, who first came to Britain from France with William the Conqueror, the castle is now cared for by a charitable trust.

Manderston House

NEAR DUNS, BORDERS

Manderston House is the home of Lord and Lady Palmer and is one of the finest Edwardian country houses in Scotland. Although somewhat restrained on the outside, the interiors are lavish beyond description and the property features the only silver staircase in the world. Originally built in the 1790s, it was recreated between 1890 and 1905 by the architect John Kinross (1855–1931) for Sir James Miller who married Evelyn Curzon, daughter of Lord Scarsdale.

St Abb's Head
BORDERS

St Abb's Head is perhaps one of the most outstanding areas of natural beauty in the Borders. Sheer cliffs sculpted from volcanic action and 192 acres of wild coastline, St Abb's Head is a National Nature Reserve and is owned by the National Trust for Scotland. The variety of seabird life is immense, including species such as Shags, Razorbills and Puffins, and the reserve is one of the most important sites of flora and fauna in the UK.

Jedburgh Abbey
BORDERS

Jedburgh Abbey was founded by King David I in 1138, although fragments remain of Celtic stonework that date back to the ninth century. The ruins of Jedburgh Abbey are situated on the north bank of the Jed Water, next to the town of Jedburgh, and are in the care of Historic Scotland. The Visitor Centre onsite tells the story of the Augustinian monks who once lived and prayed there. Of particular interest is the shape of the great rose window on the western front.

Traquair House

NEAR PEEBLES, BORDERS

Traquair House dates back to 1107 and was a Stuart Stronghold for 500 years; Mary Queen of Scots being one of the many monarchs to have stayed there. Nowadays the grand property provides bed and breakfast accommodation and is popular as a business and wedding venue. The extensive grounds, maze, craft workshop and the brewery make Traquair House a special and particularly romantic place.

Melrose Abbey

BORDERS

Melrose is considered to be the finest of the Border's four abbeys. A
magnificent ruin, it was originally built in 1136 for the Cistercian order.
In 1385, it was burned to the ground by the English army, but rose
again from the ashes as a stunning, ornate fifteenth-century place of
worship, representing one of the wealthiest monasteries in Scotland.
Within the grounds is a commemorative plaque of Robert the Bruce,
whose heart is believed to be buried here. The ruins are cared for by
Historic Scotland.